Copyright © Year 2025

All Rights Reserved by **Valerie Jones.**

No part of this publication may be reproduced in any form, or by any means, electronic or mechanical, including photocopying, recording, or any information browsing, storage, or retrieval system, without permission in writing from Valerie Jones.

ISBN
Hardcover: 979-8-90190-084-0
Paperback: 979-8-90190-083-3

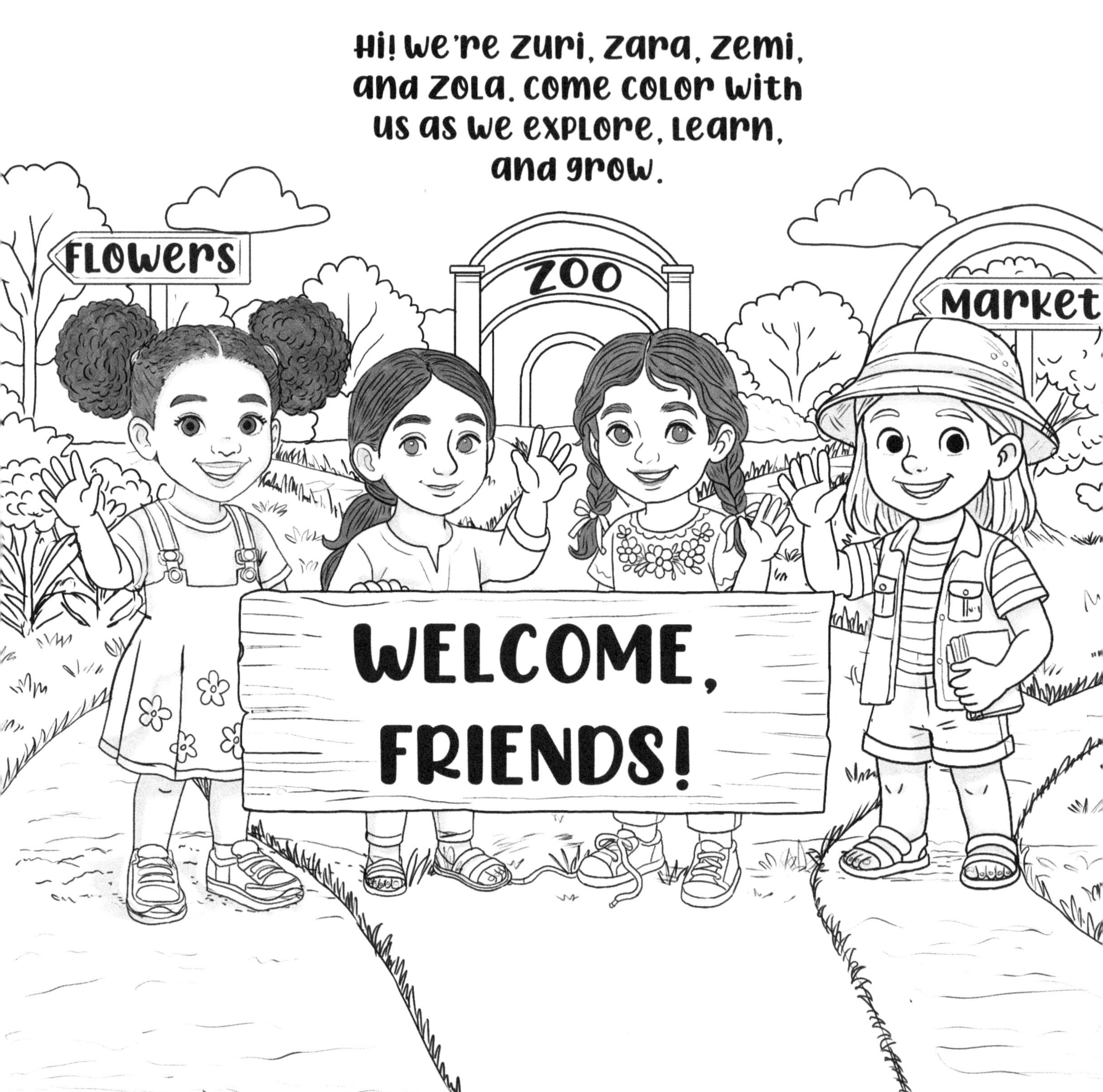

Hi! We're Zuri, Zara, Zemi, and Zola. Come color with us as we explore, learn, and grow.
FLOWERS
ZOO
Market
WELCOME, FRIENDS!

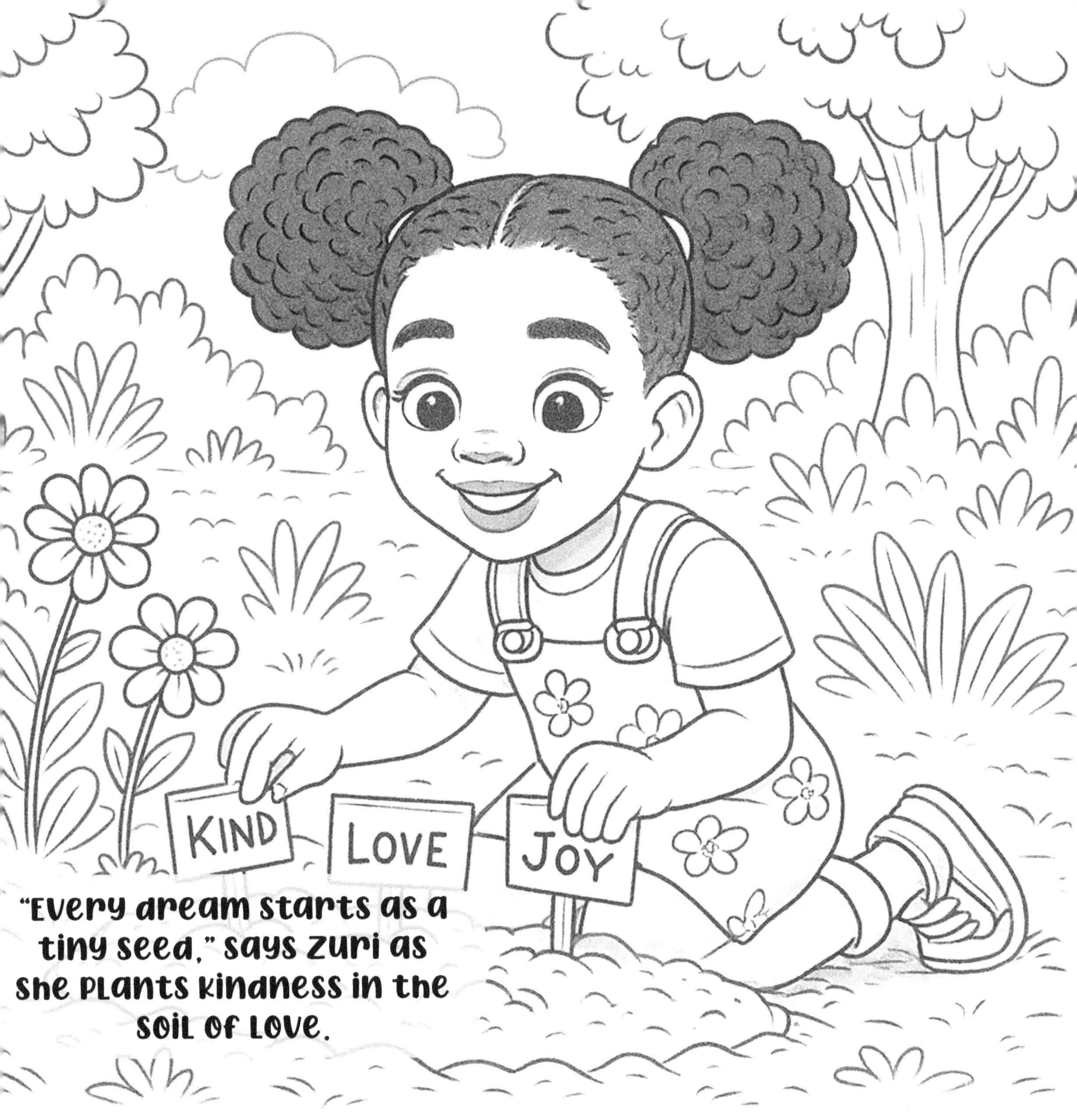

"Every dream starts as a tiny seed," says Zuri as she plants kindness in the soil of love.

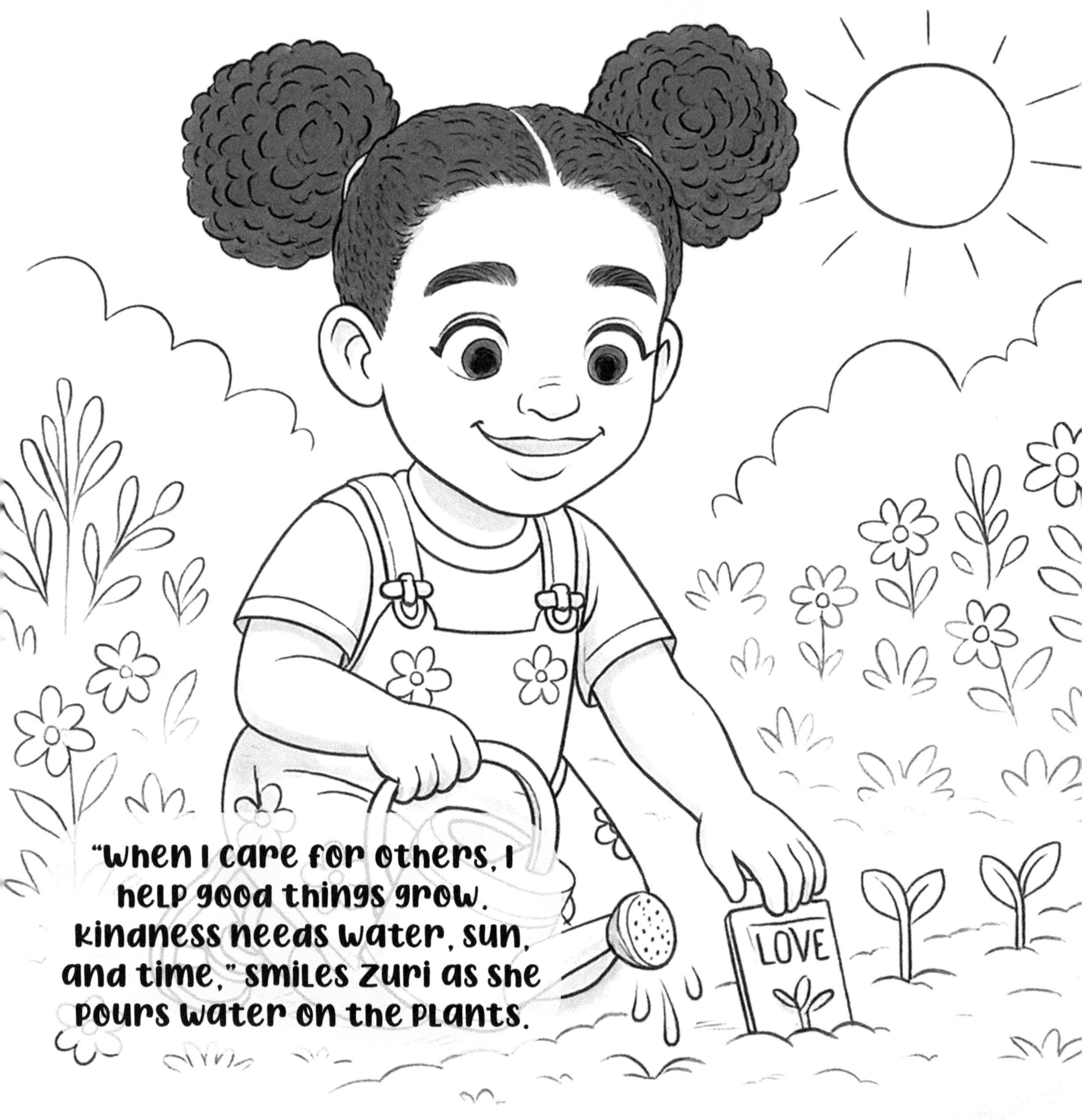

"When I care for others, I help good things grow. Kindness needs water, sun, and time," smiles Zuri as she pours water on the plants.
LOVE

"I am brave, even when I feel small. My words can plant hope in others," Zuri continues.

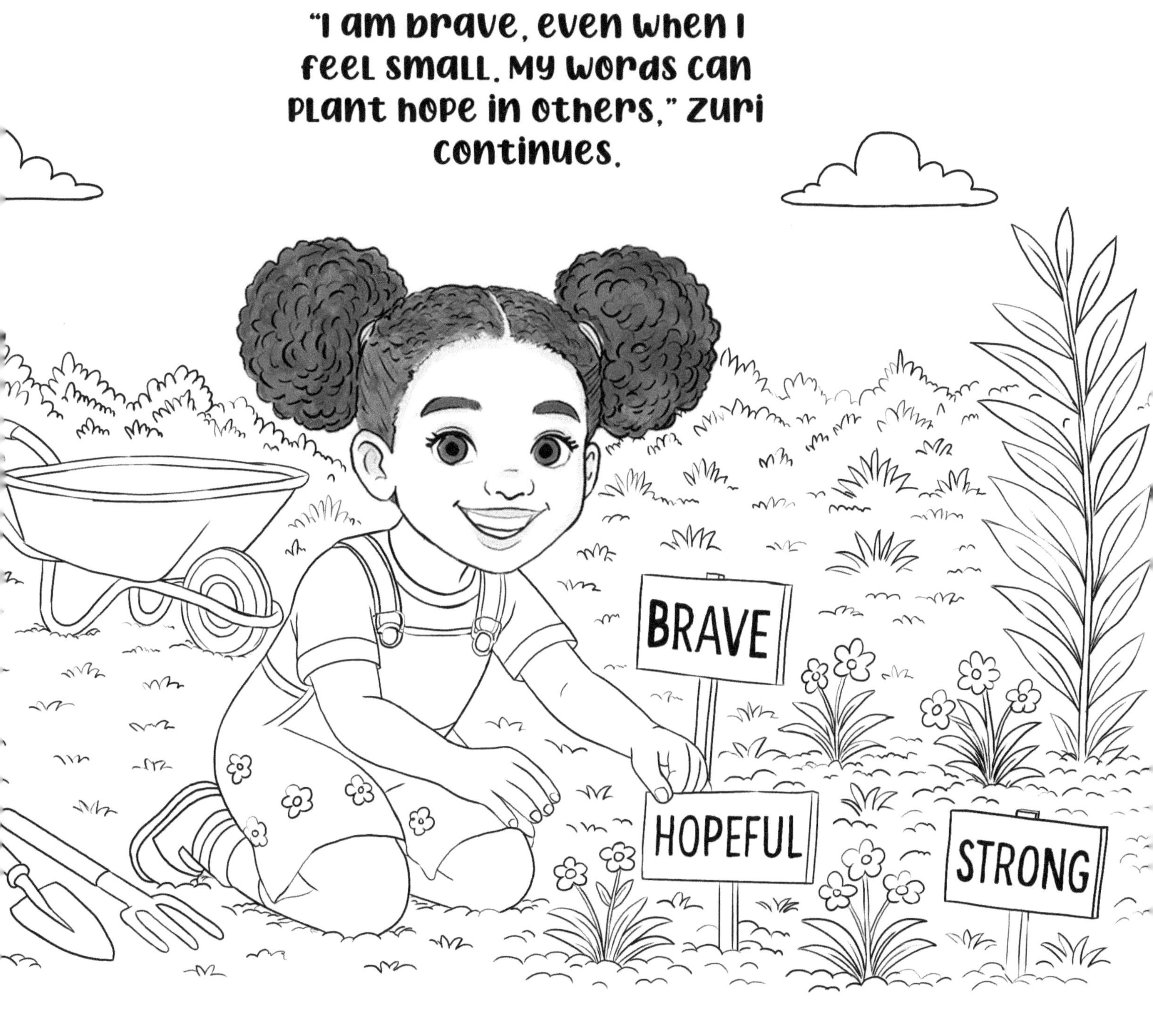

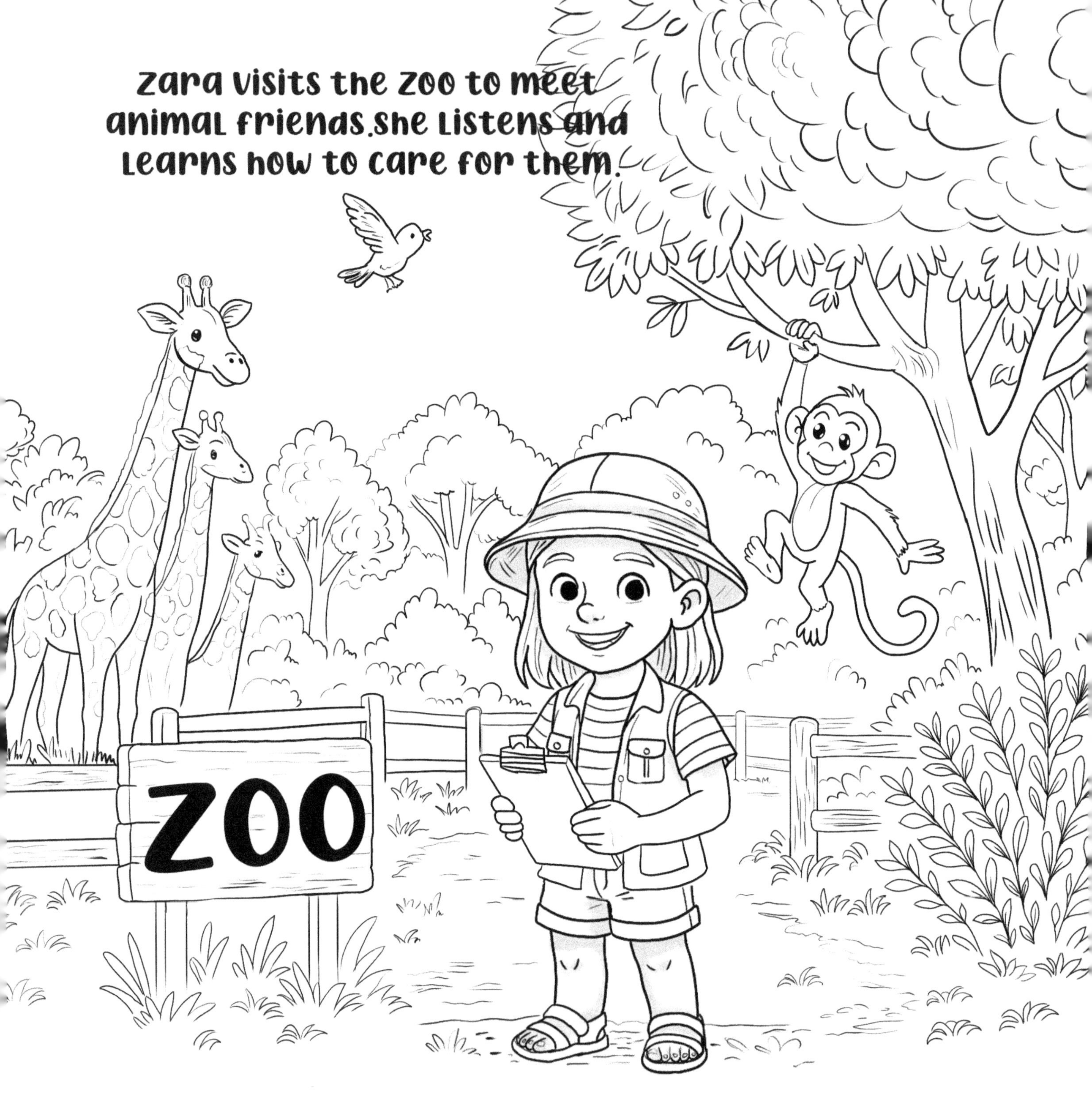

zara visits the zoo to meet animal friends.she listens and learns how to care for them.
ZOO

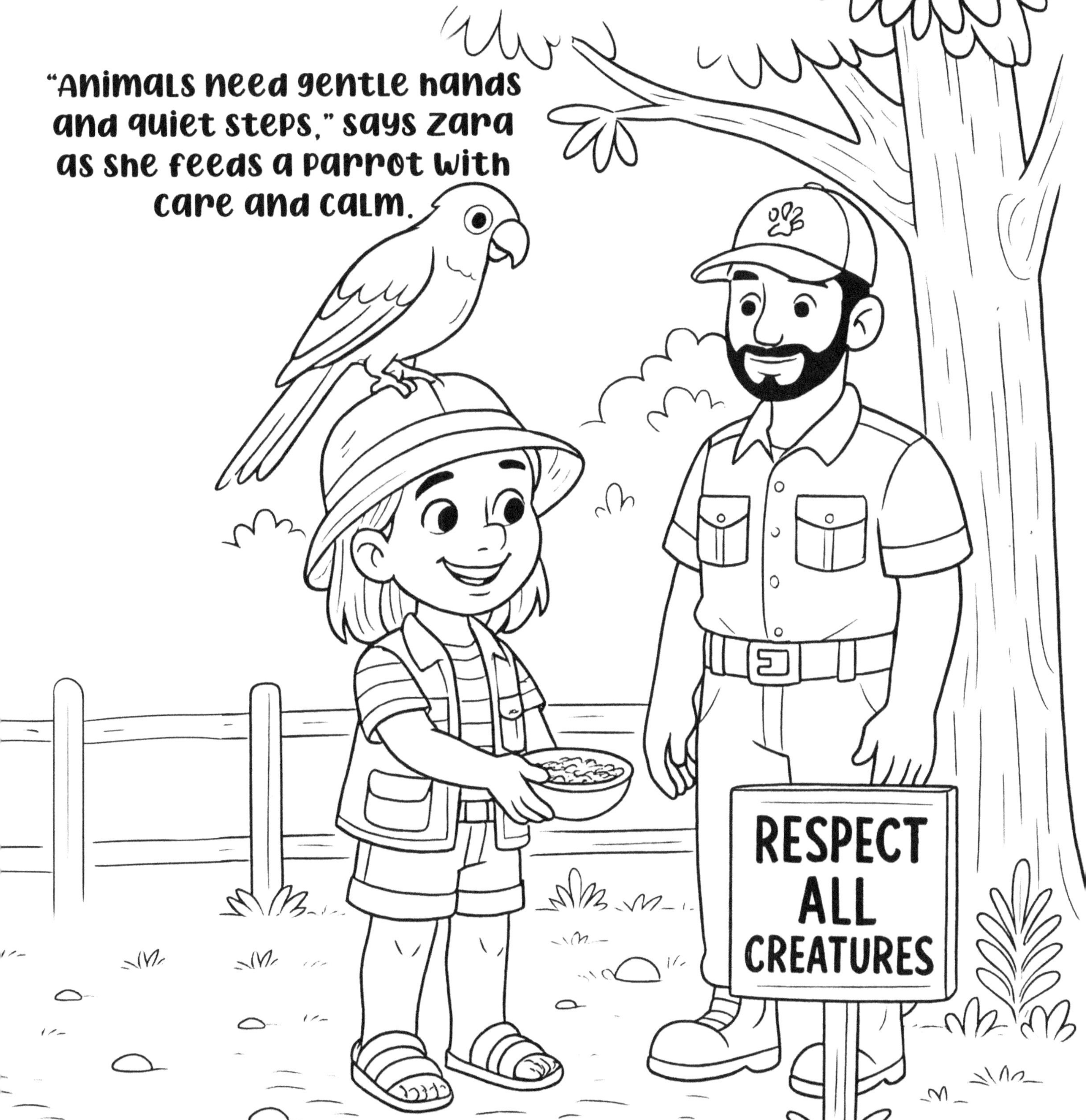

"Animals need gentle hands and quiet steps," says Zara as she feeds a parrot with care and calm.
RESPECT ALL CREATURES

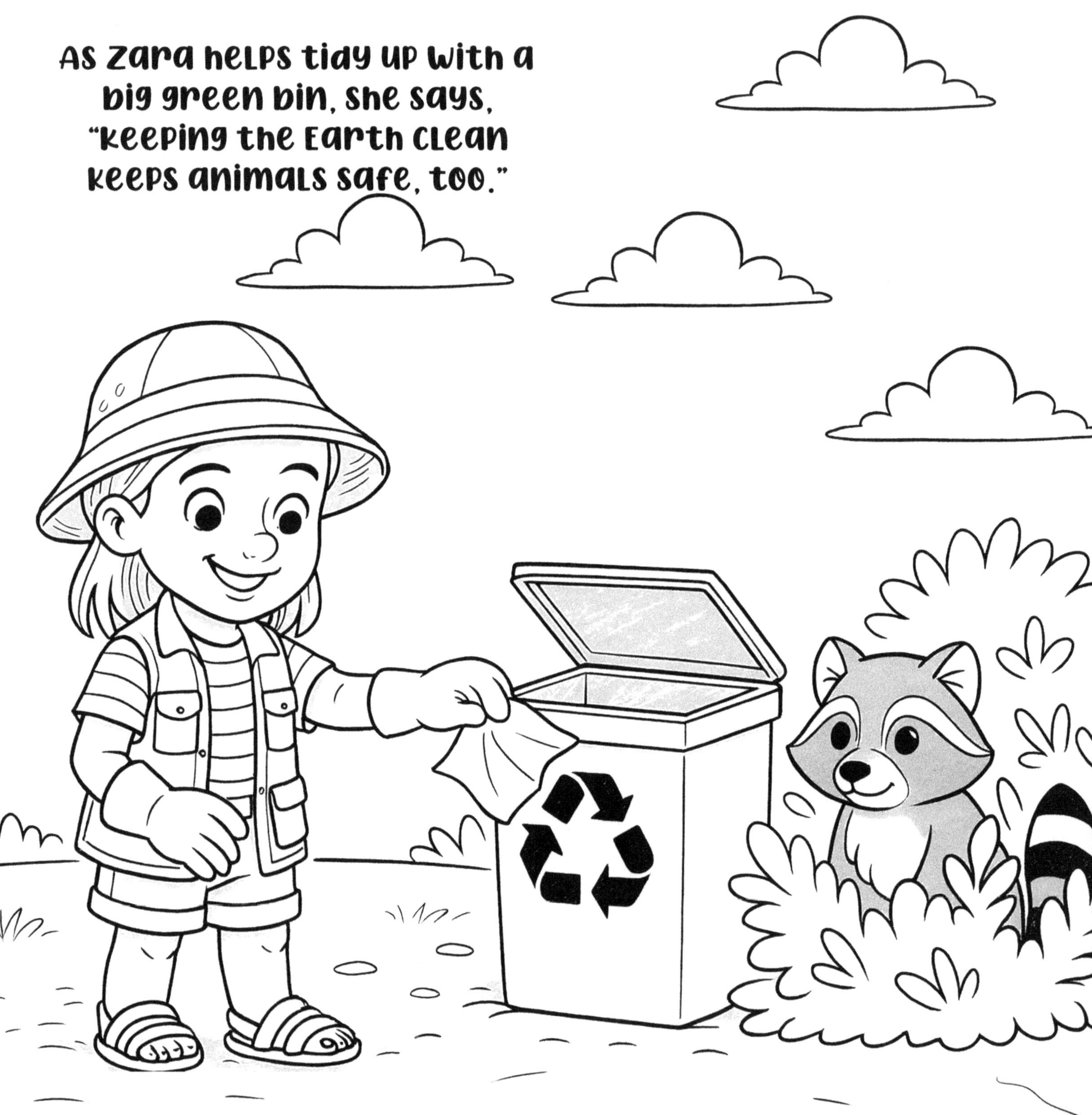

As Zara helps tidy up with a big green bin, she says, "Keeping the Earth clean keeps animals safe, too."

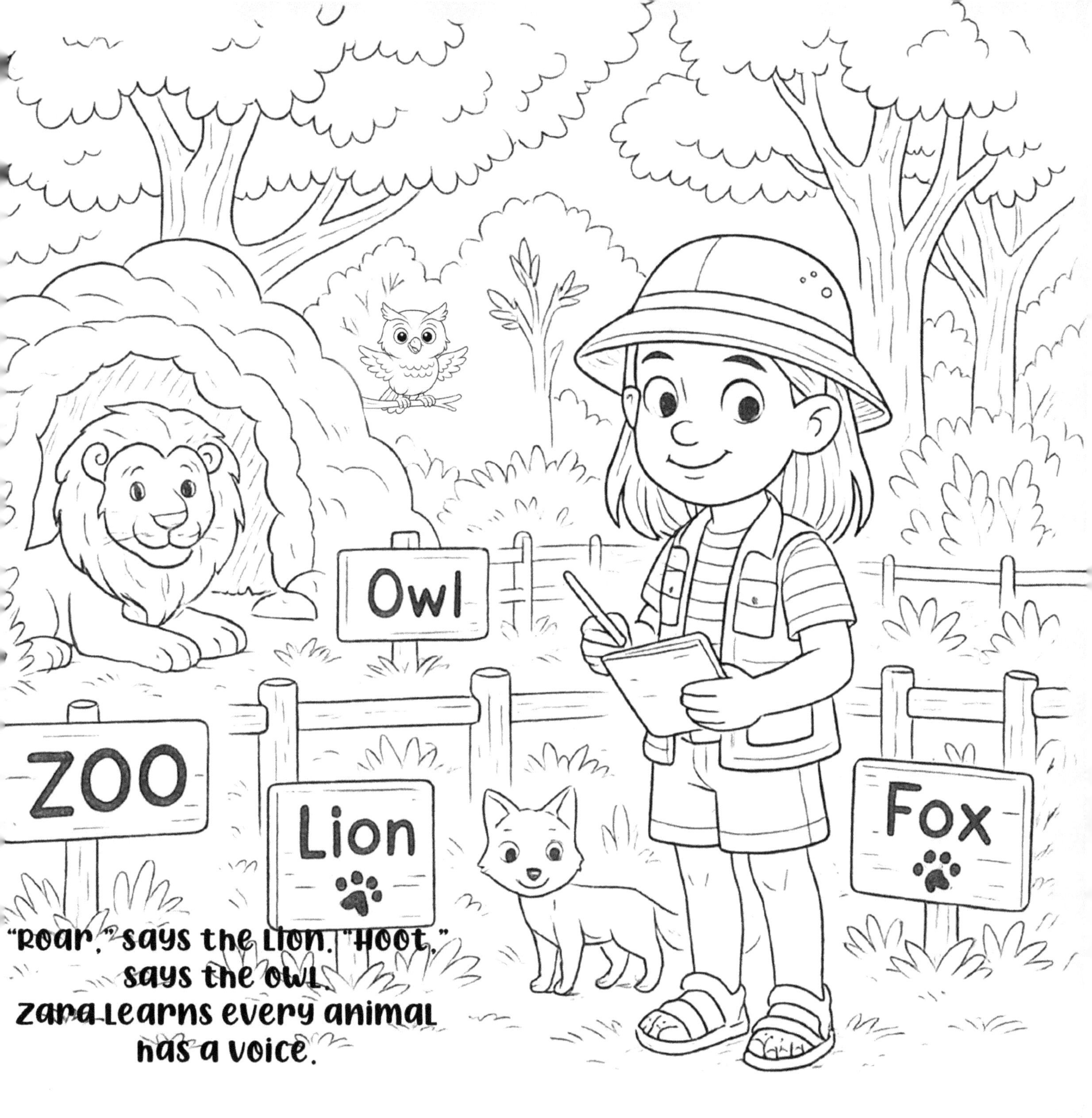

"Roar," says the Lion. "Hoot,"
says the Owl.
Zara learns every animal
has a voice.

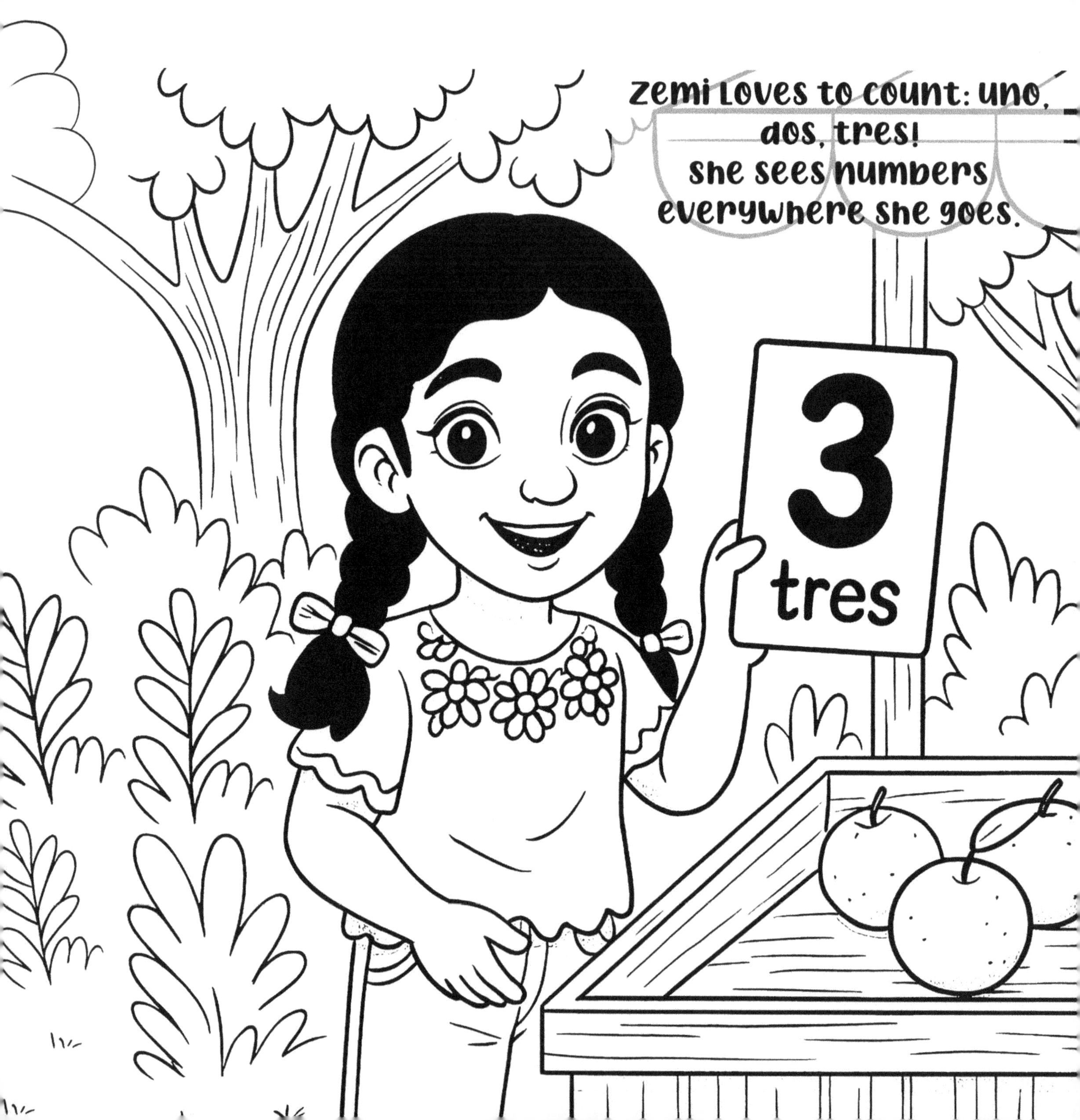

Zemi loves to count: uno, dos, tres!
She sees numbers everywhere she goes.
3
tres

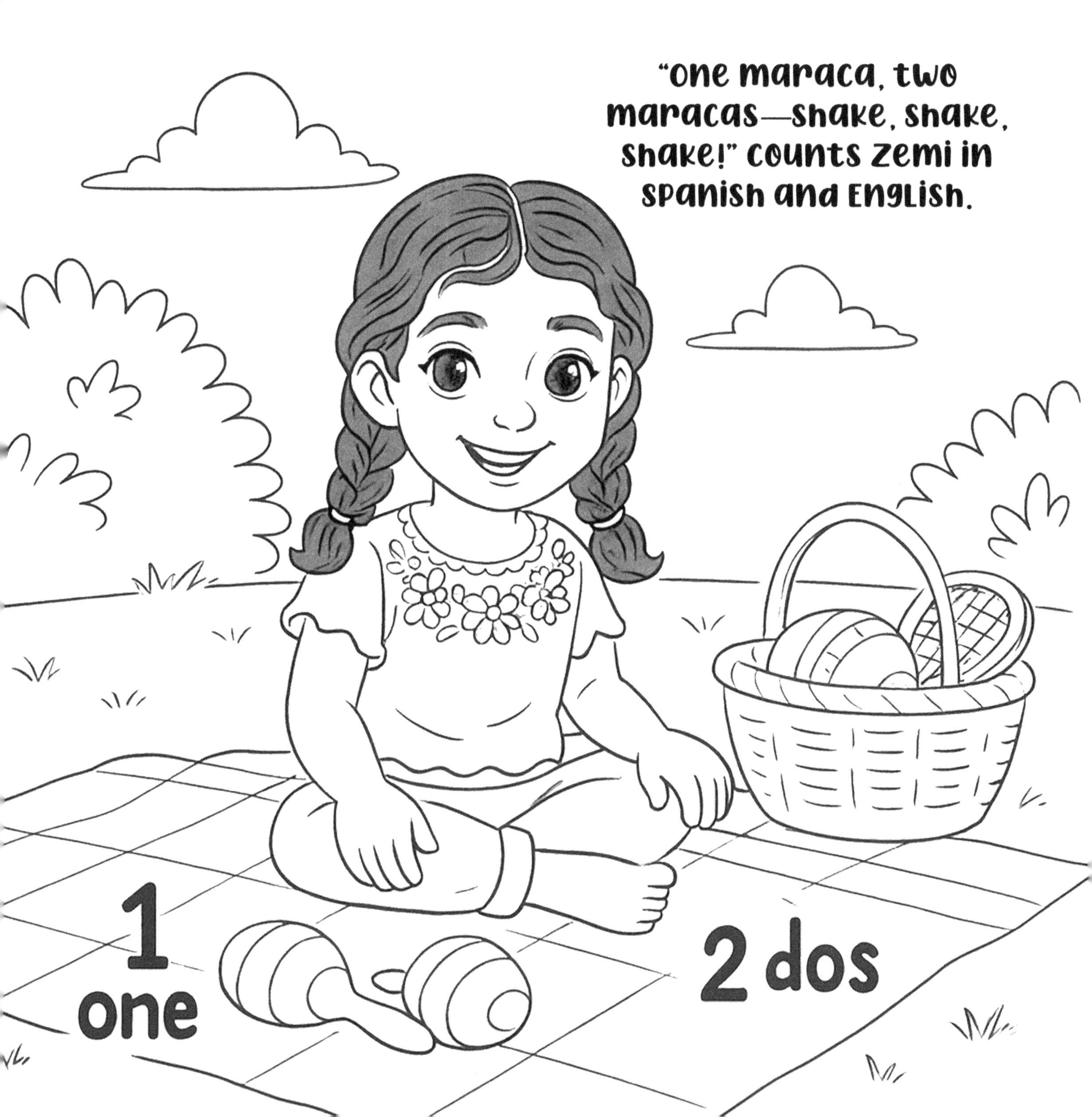

"one maraca, two maracas—shake, shake, shake!" counts Zemi in Spanish and English.
1
one
2 dos

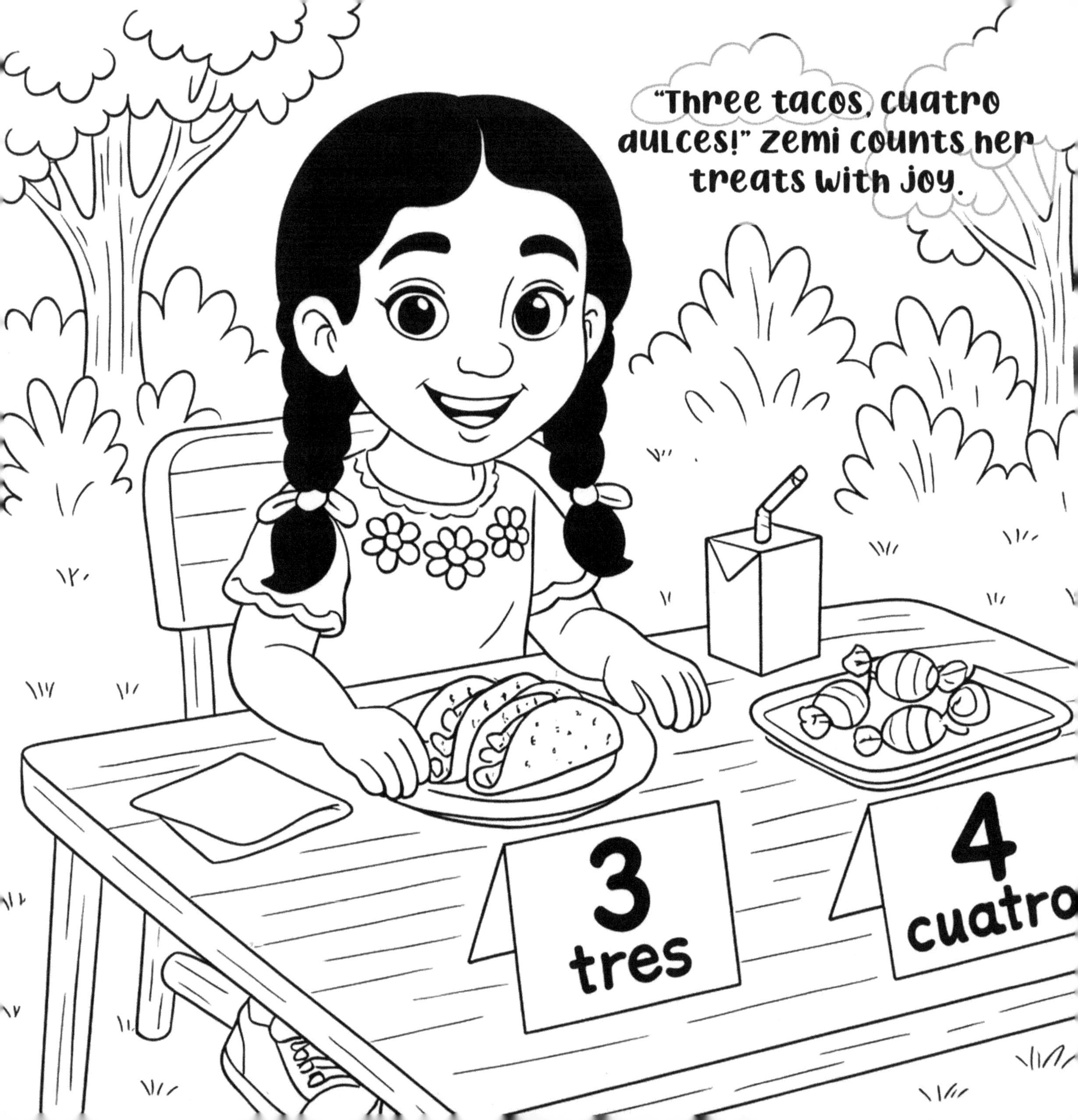

"Three tacos, cuatro dulces!" Zemi counts her treats with joy.
3 tres
4 cuatro

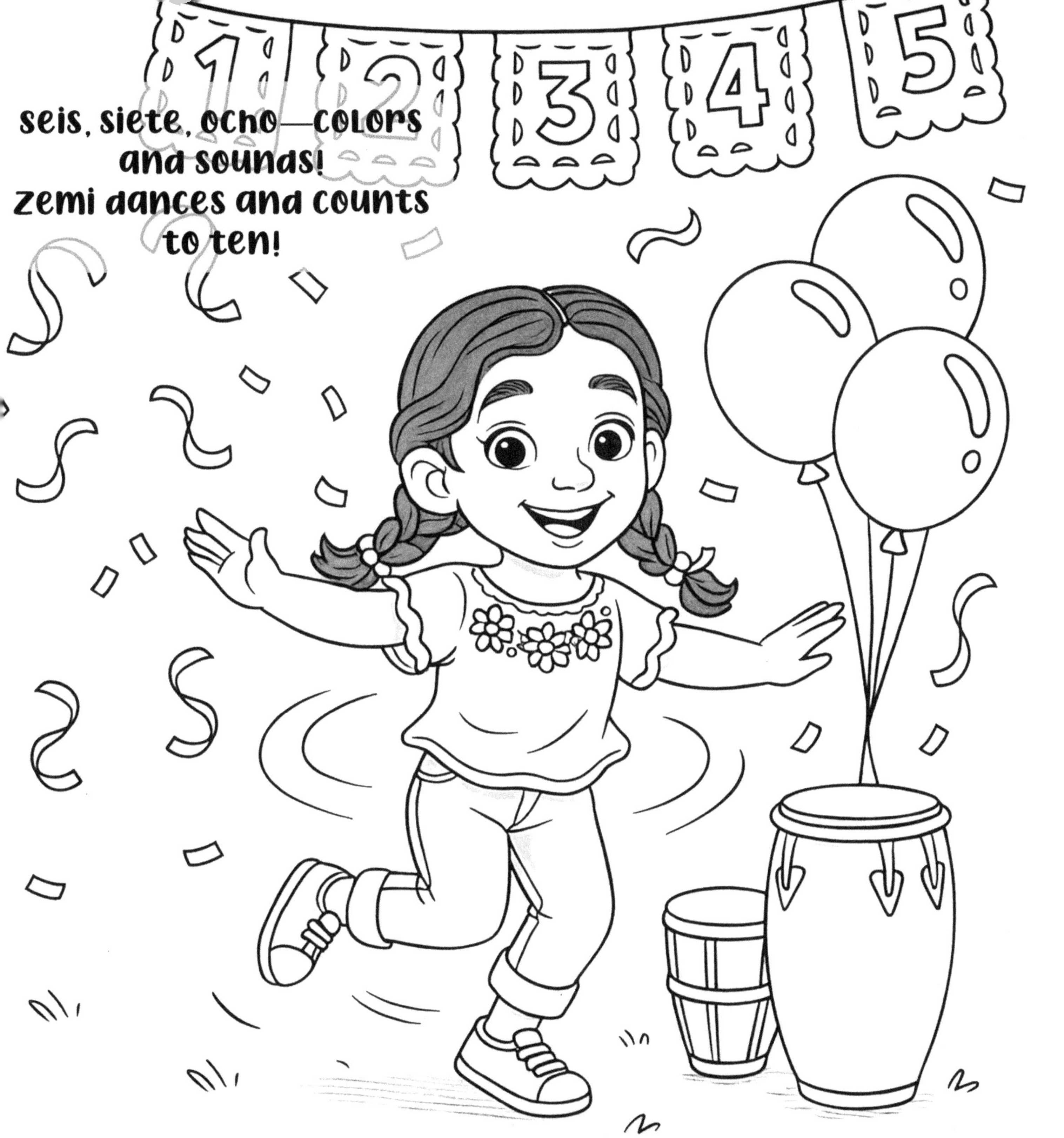

1 2 3 4 5
seis, siete, ocho—colors and sounds!
Zemi dances and counts to ten!

Zola sees colors in every feeling.
Red for love, blue for calm, yellow for joy!

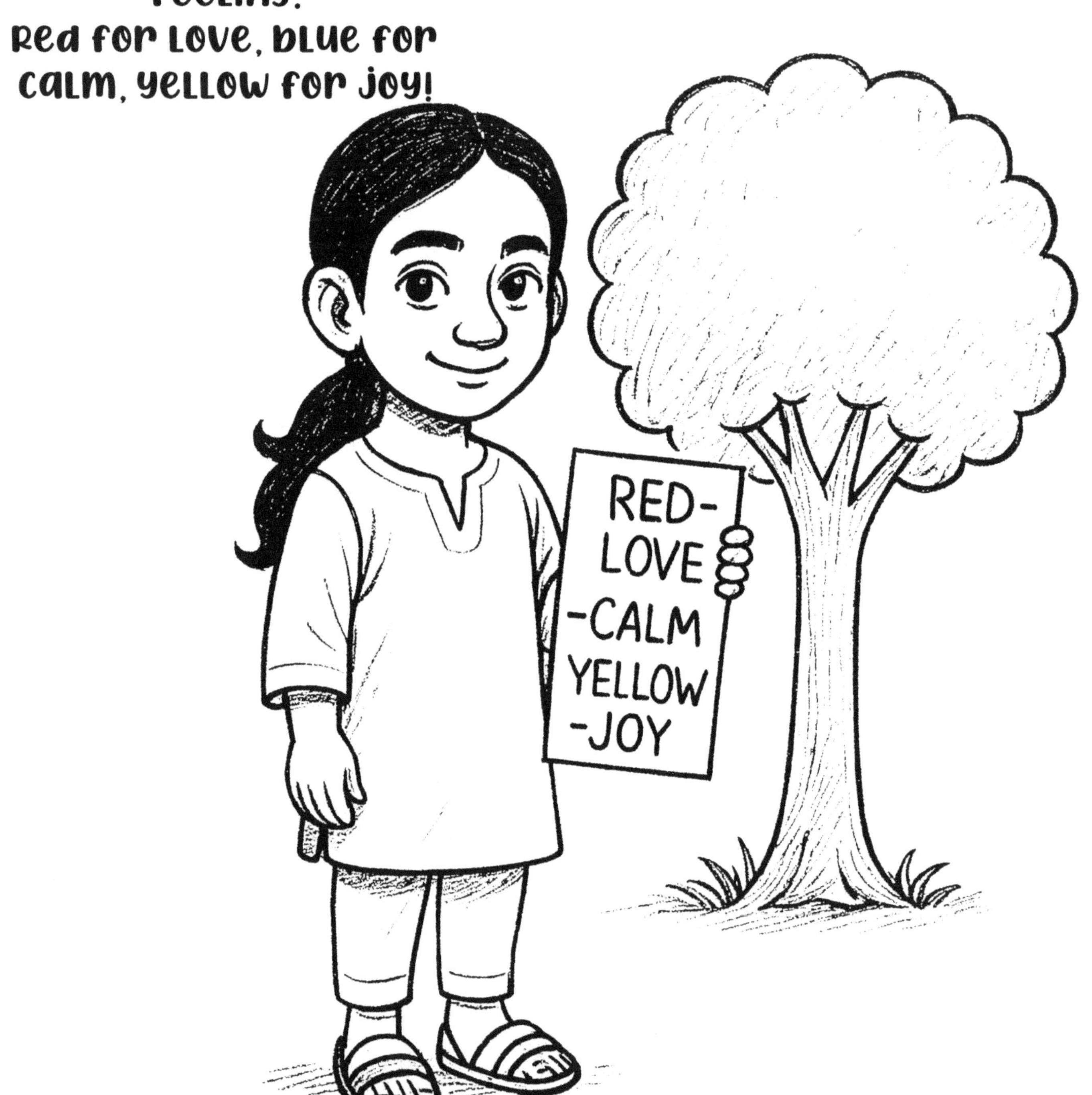

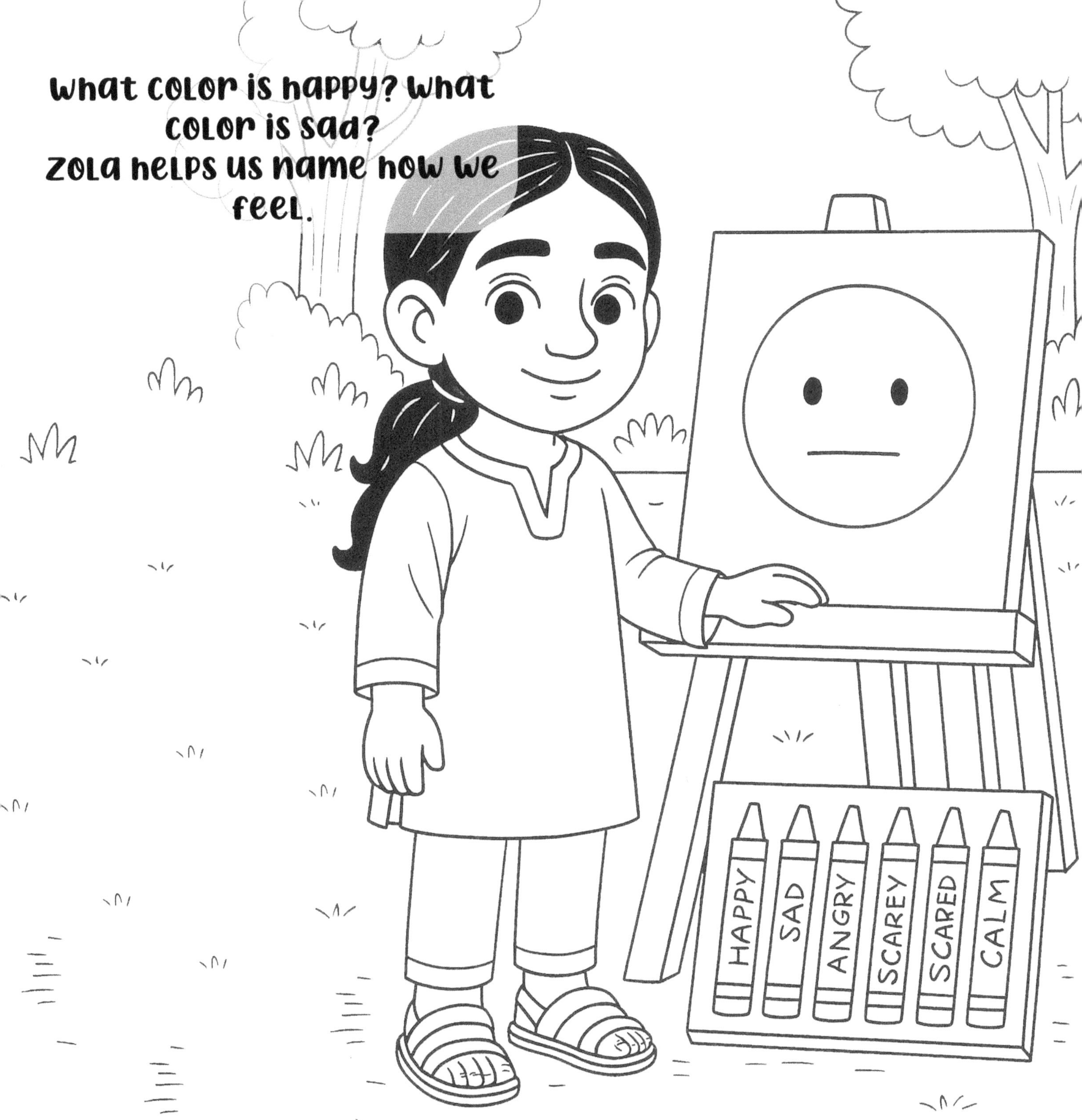

what color is happy? what color is sad?
zola helps us name how we feel.
HAPPY
SAD
ANGRY
SCAREY
SCARED
CALM

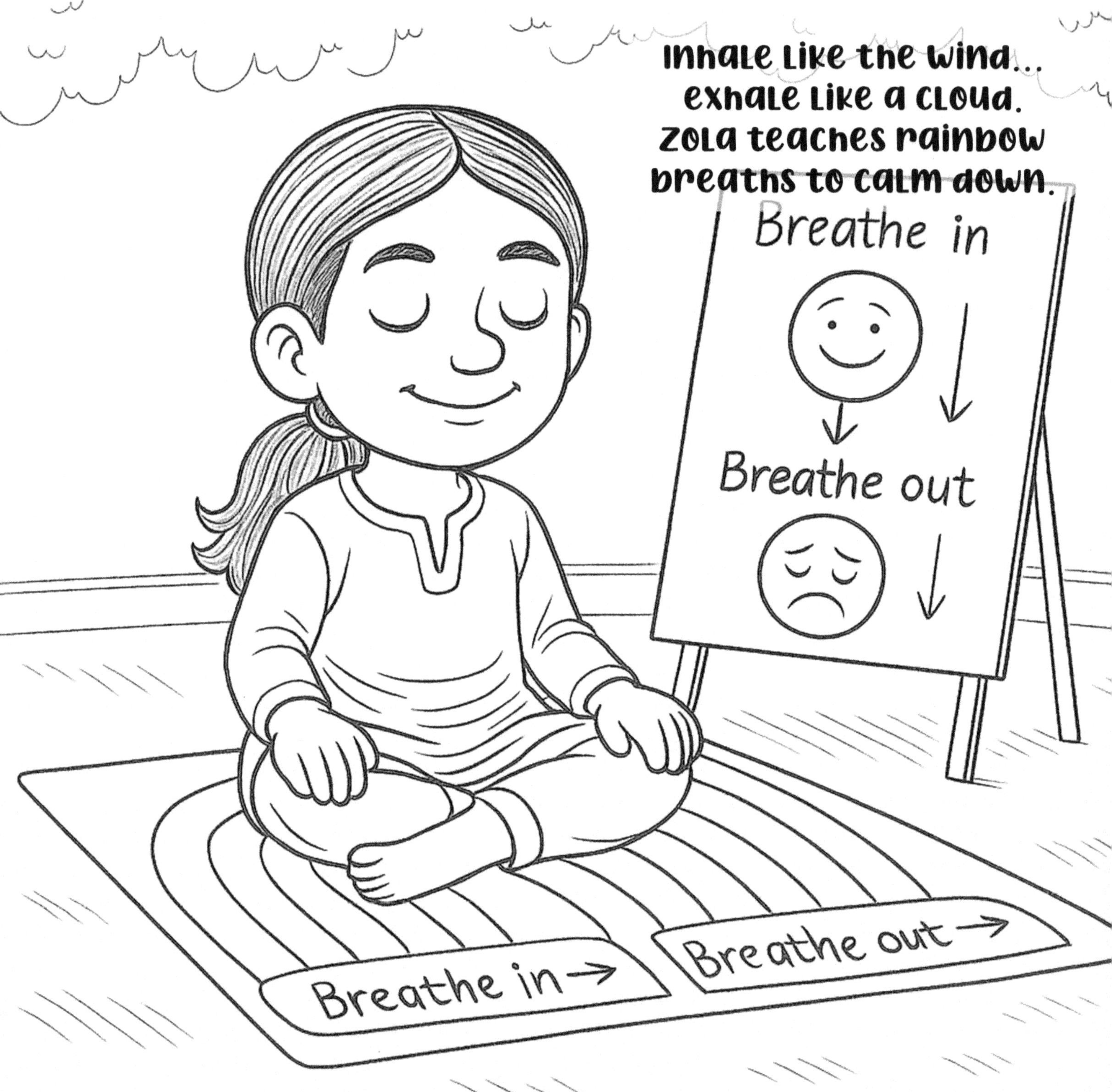

Inhale like the wind...
exhale like a cloud.
Zola teaches rainbow
breaths to calm down.
Breathe in
Breathe out
Breathe in →
Breathe out →

"Sometimes I feel big feelings inside," Zola says. "It's okay to feel them all," she continues.

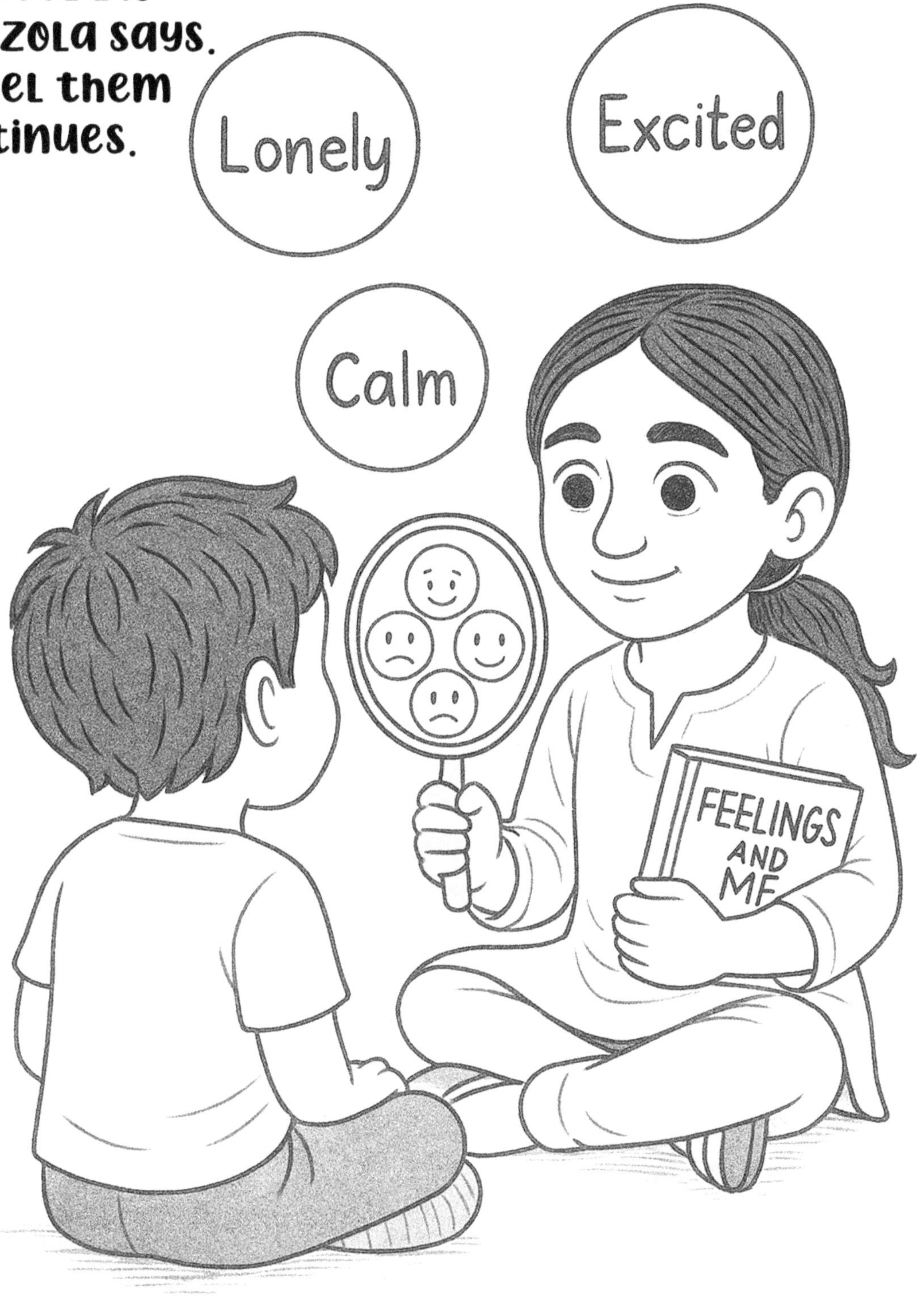

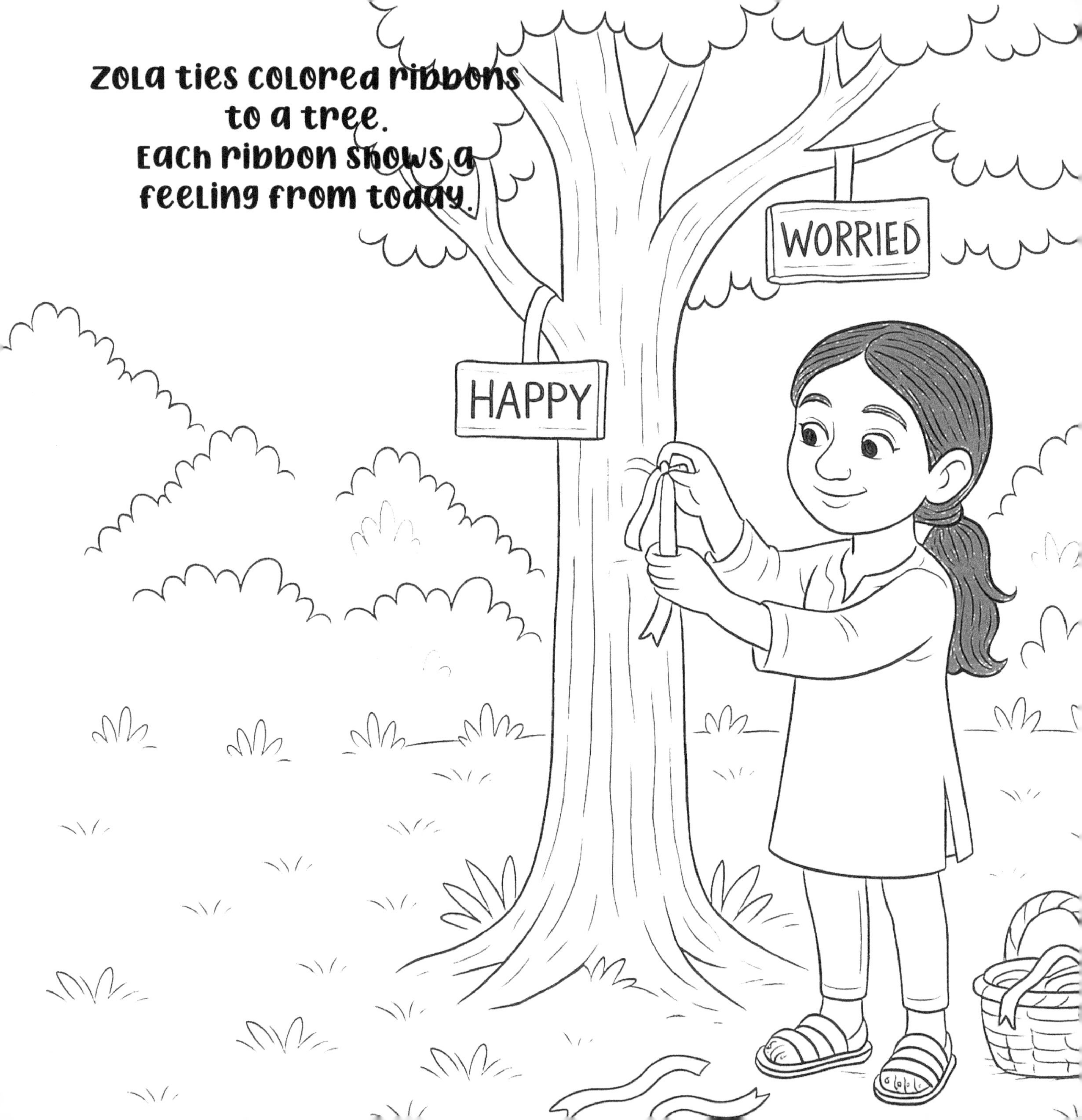

Zola ties colored ribbons to a tree. Each ribbon shows a feeling from today.
WORRIED
HAPPY

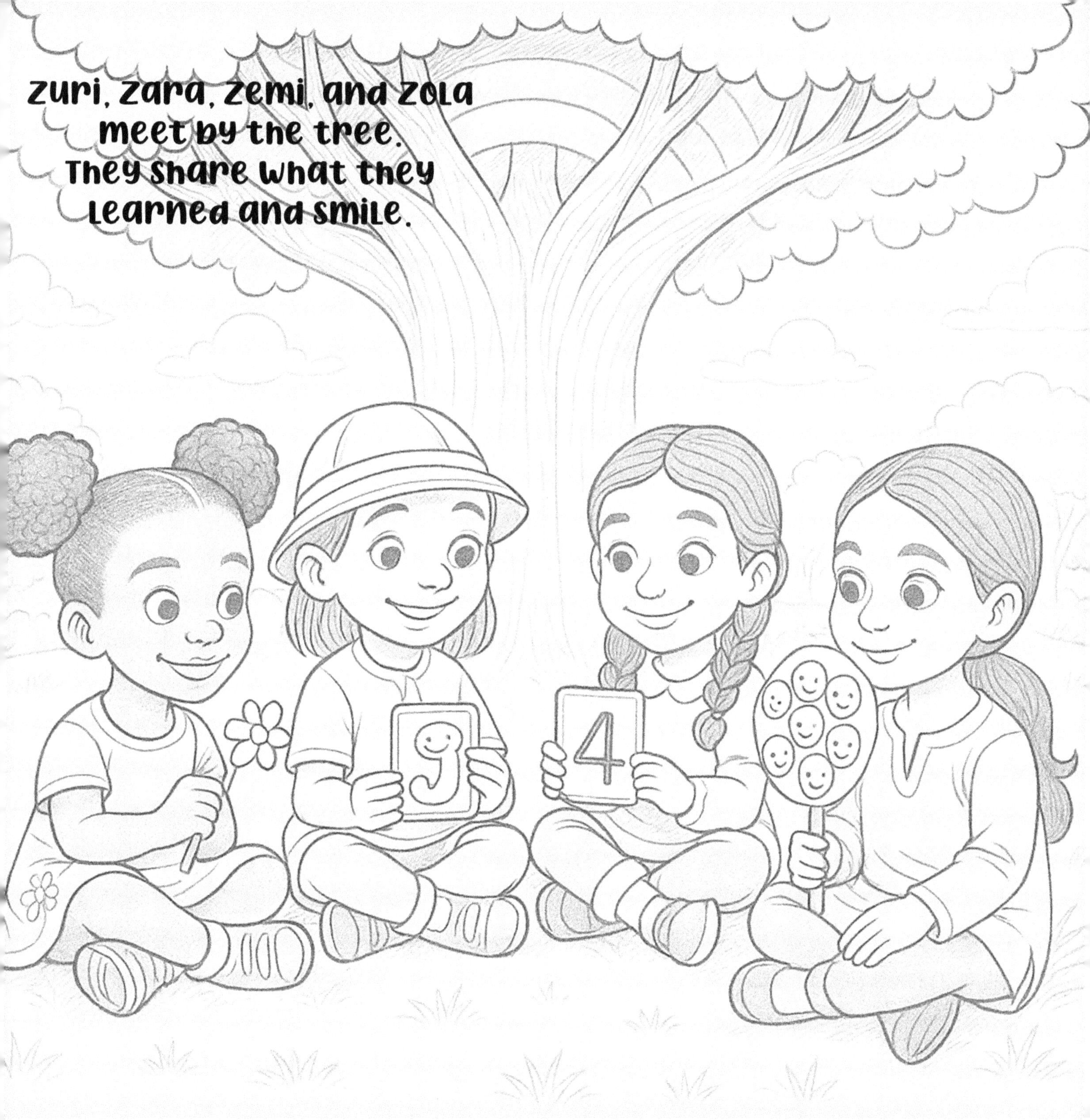

Zuri, Zara, Zemi, and Zola
meet by the tree.
They share what they
learned and smile.

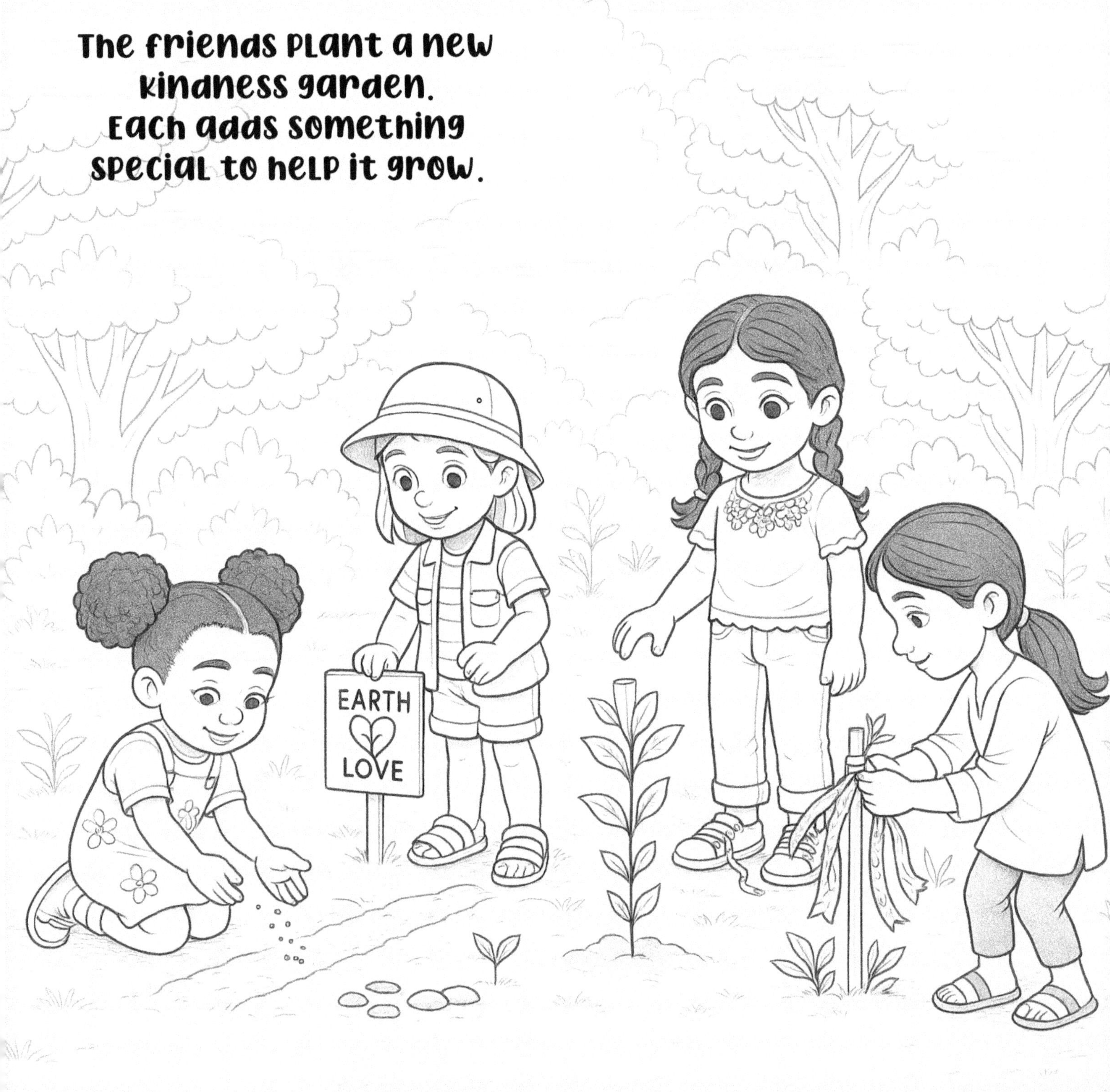

The friends plant a new kindness garden.
Each adds something special to help it grow.
EARTH
LOVE

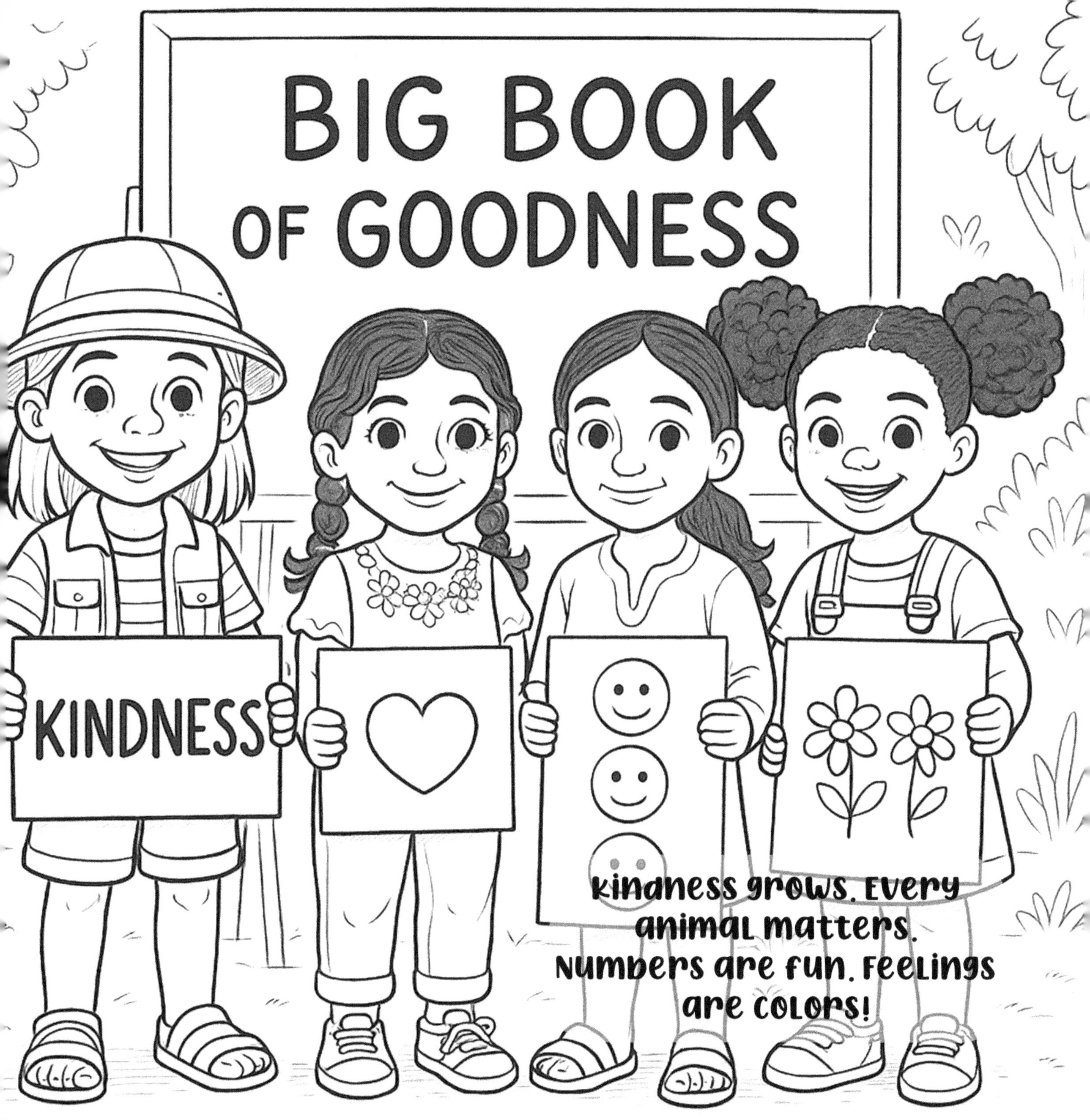

BIG BOOK
OF GOODNESS
KINDNESS
Kindness grows. Every
animal matters.
Numbers are fun. Feelings
are colors!

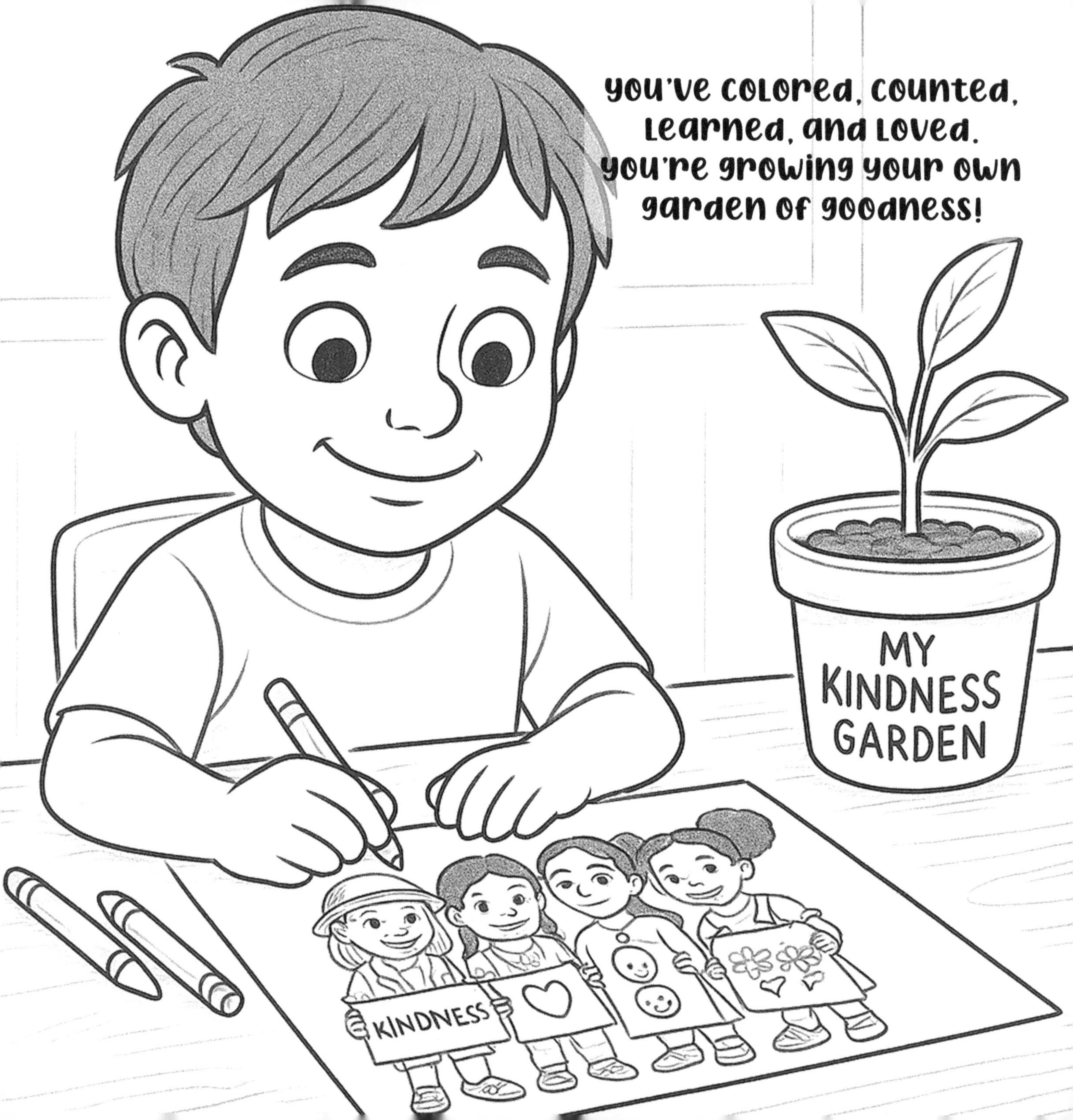

You've colored, counted, learned, and loved. You're growing your own garden of goodness!
MY KINDNESS GARDEN
KINDNESS

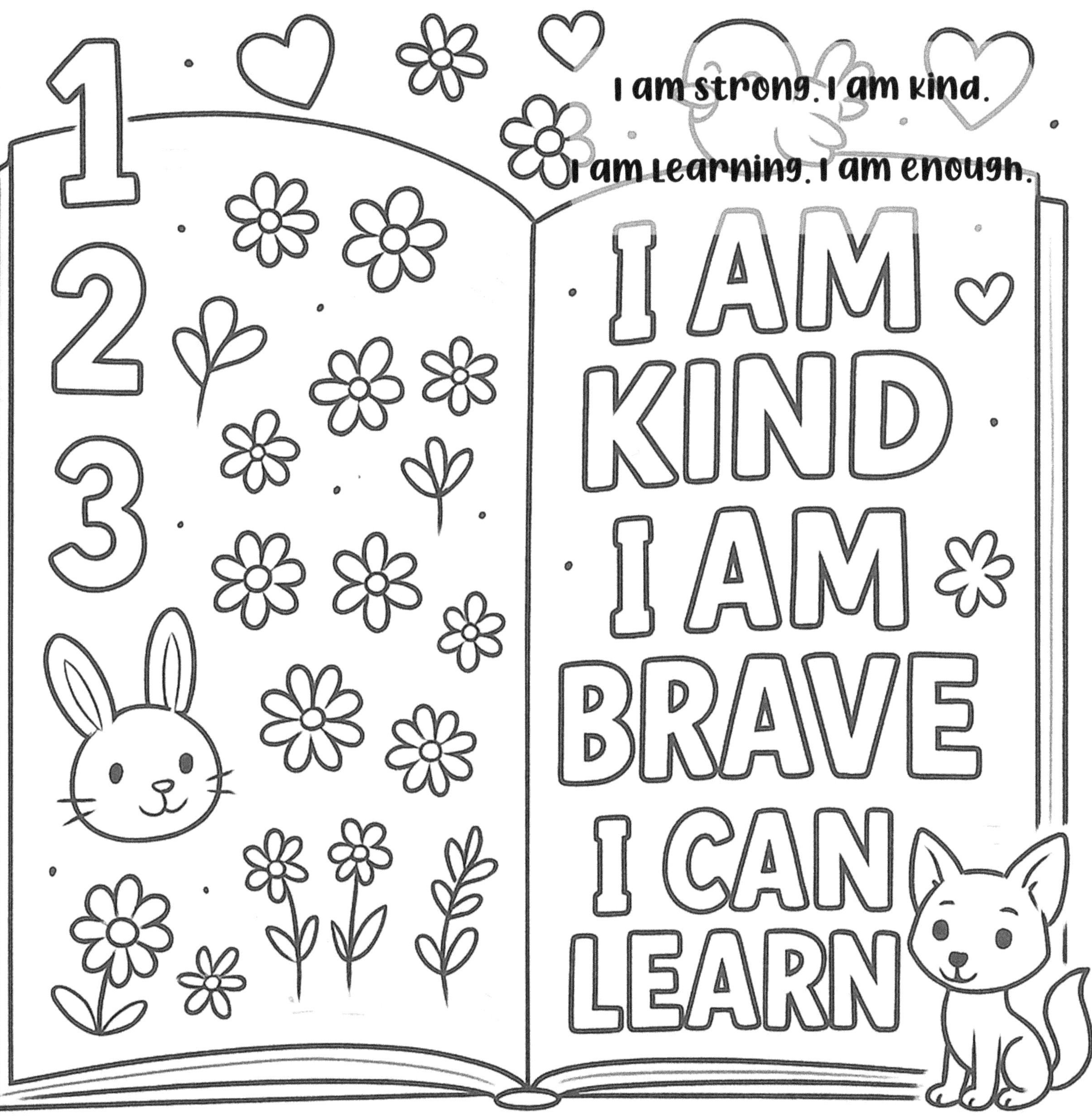

1
2
3
I am strong. I am kind.
I am Learning. I am enough.
I AM
KIND
I AM
BRAVE
I CAN
LEARN

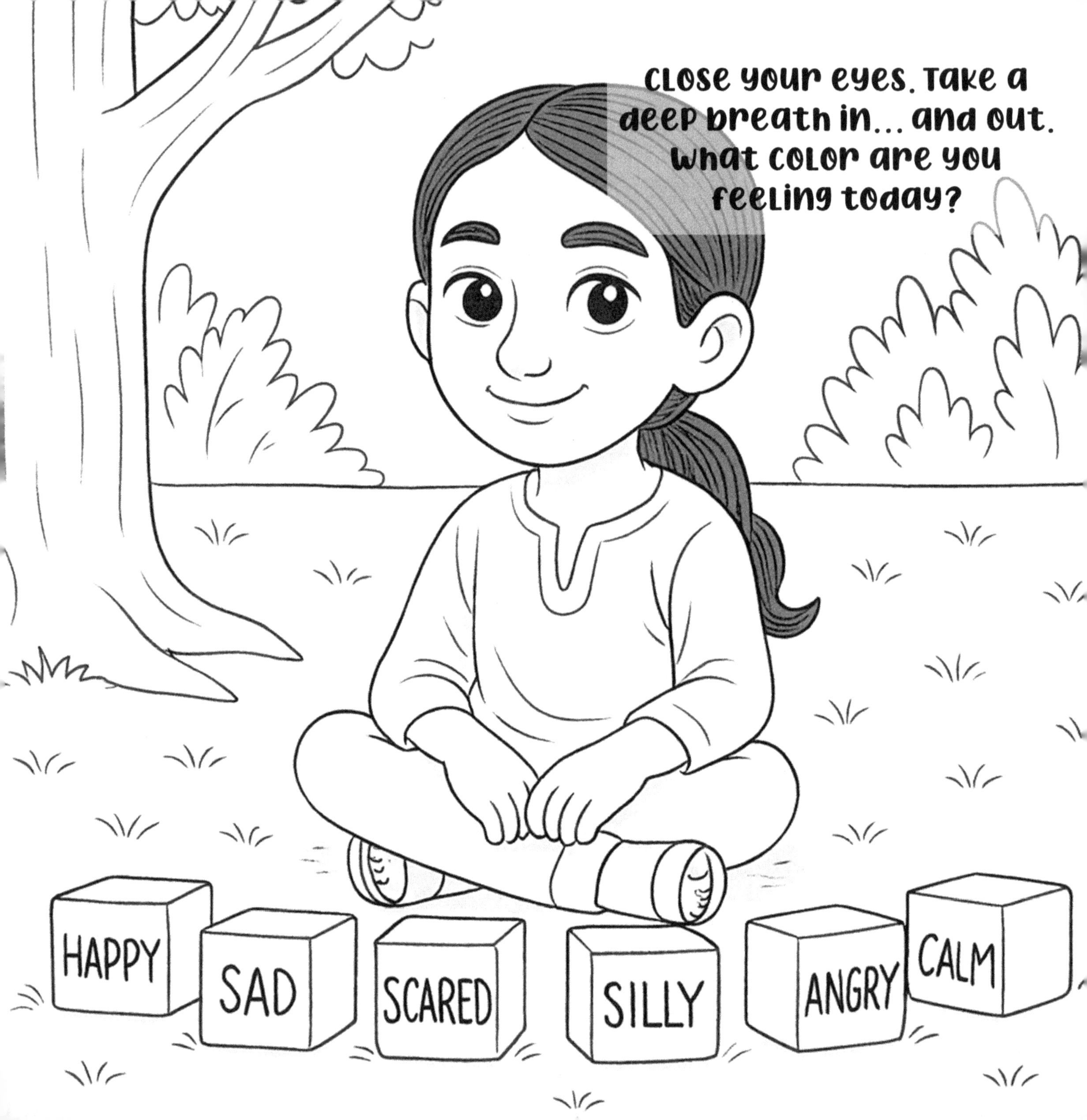

Close your eyes. Take a deep breath in… and out. What color are you feeling today?
HAPPY
SAD
SCARED
SILLY
ANGRY
CALM

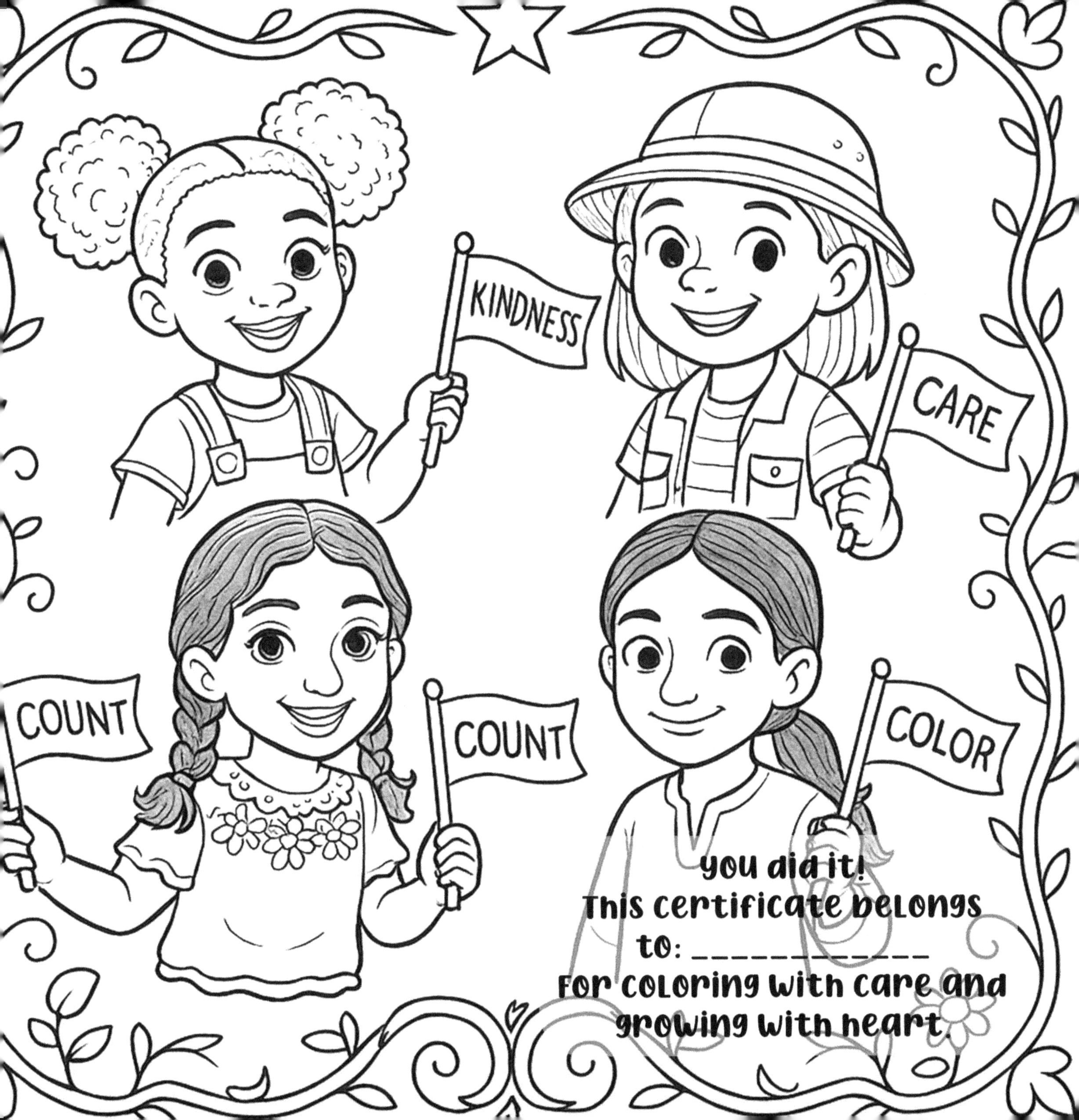

KINDNESS
CARE
COUNT
COUNT
COLOR
You did it!
This certificate belongs to: _______________
For coloring with care and growing with heart